1 John 4: 1.1
Chapter 37.

WISDOM

on Life

RICHARD C. HALVERSON

VISION™ HOUSE PUBLISHING, INC.

Gresham, Oregon 97030

WISDOM ON LIFE
© 1994 by Richard C. Halverson

Published by Vision House Publishing, Inc.

Edited by Chip MacGregor
Cover Design by Multnomah Graphics
Interior Design by Martin Bogan

Printed in the United States of America

International Standard Book Number: 1-885305-11-7

Vision House Publishing, Inc.
1217 N.E. Burnside Road, Suite 403
Gresham, Oregon 97030

Scripture references are from:

New American Standard Bible, The Lockman Foundation © 1960, 1962, 1963, 1968, 1971, 1972, 1973, 1975, 1977. Used by permission.
New International Version, © 1973, 1978, 1984 by International Bible Society. Used by permission of Zondervan Publishing House.
All rights reserved. The "NIV" and "New International Version" trademarks are registered in the United States Patent and Trademark Office by International Bible Society. Use of either trademark requires the permission of International Bible Society.
Revised Standard Version of the Bible, © 1946, 1952, 1971, 1973, Division of Christian Education, National Council of Churches of Christ in the USA. Used by permission.
J. B. Phillips: The New Testament in Modern English, J. B. Phillips © 1958. Used by permission of Macmillan Publishing Co., Inc.
The Good News Bible in Today's English Version, © 1983. Used by permission of Thomas Nelson, Inc.

94 95 96 97 98 99 00 01 02 03 — 10 9 8 7 6 5 4 3 2 1

When is a winner a loser…

And when is a loser a winner?

Competing against others is not the big contest in life.

Competing with oneself is the big one!

Alexander the Great conquered the world…

And cursed his own lack of self control.

A winner is a loser — no matter how many victories to his credit — *if he has lost the battle with himself.*

A loser is a winner — however many his losses — if he conquers himself.

In fact, *his losses may contribute to his victory over self more than any other factor.*

In our culture we're conditioned to win — never lose.

Despite the fact that for every winner in a contest between two or more, there has to be a loser.

We have great difficulty in handling a loss...

Which is a strong factor in gaining the victory over self.

But the victory over another may be the very thing that contributes to the winner's failure to conquer himself.

Winning makes him proud, arrogant, independent, thoughtless, and sometimes cruel.

To put it another way — it isn't what happens to you, *but how you handle what happens that makes the difference.*

Jesus said, "If any one will be my disciple, let him deny himself... and follow me."

— Luke 9:23

The first two recorded questions in the Bible were asked by God of man. Implicit in which is the root of all conflict in history.

The first: "Adam, where are you?"

— Genesis 3:9

God knew — *but Adam had to respond.*

Adam was hiding from God — that is sin in its most basic sense! A violation of God's unconditional love.

Second: "Where is Abel your brother?"

— Genesis 4:9

Cain had killed his brother — that is the consequence of rejecting God's love.

"I was afraid," Adam said.

Afraid of God? Afraid of Him Who in love created man for fellowship with Himself? Afraid of Him Who desires man's perfection and fulfillment? *Afraid of Him who is consummate love?*

That is the genesis of all fear, all hatred, all hostility, all alienation, all conflict.

"Am I my brother's keeper?"

Implicit in that question is *rejection of the fundamental relationship in the human family*.

I am my brother's keeper in the divine economy!

To love God, not fear Him... to love fellow man, not destroy him, encompasses all the law and all the prophets.

That is to be human in sublime perfection... violation of which is the genesis of all evil!

"Beloved, let us love one another; for love is of God, and he who loves is born of God and knows God. He who does not love does not know God; for God is love."

— I John 4:7-8

"If anyone says, 'I love God,' and hates his brother, he is a liar; for he who does not love his brother whom he has seen, cannot love God Whom he has not seen."

— I John 4:20

— 3 —

The golden text...

"God so loved the world that He gave His only begotten Son that whosoever believeth on Him should not perish but have everlasting life".

— John 3:16

God is...

The Bible makes no attempt to prove God — no argument, no debate. It simply begins with God — the ultimate Reality.

God loves...

Unconditionally — eternally — relentlessly — "God is love."

The world...

Universal love — all people — everywhere — no exceptions — every race, language, tribe, color, and nation included.

That He gave...

Love is active — love gives.

His Son...

The best He had to offer — the inexpressible Gift — the supreme Gift — the total Gift. He gave Himself in His Son.

Whosoever...

God is perfectly impartial — no one excluded.

Believeth on Him...

That is accepts — trusts — takes Him at His word.

Should not perish...

A glorious future unmarred by guilt or judgment.

Have everlasting life...

Enemy death conquered — life unending.

4

"As a man thinketh in his heart so is he."

Put it in more contemporary terms: "Man becomes what he thinks about all day long."

It's mighty important how one thinks.

Important also to realize that the worldly way of thinking is exactly opposite to God's.

"My thoughts are not your thoughts, said the Lord, neither are My ways your ways; but as high as the heaven above the earth are My thoughts above your thoughts and My ways above yours."

— Isaiah 55: 8-9

From God's point of view to be great one must become a servant.

To be exalted, one must humble himself...

To receive, one must give...

To be happy, one must mourn...

To seek one's life, one must lose it...

To lose one's life is to find it.

From the human standpoint, this is crazy...

But it is the way of wisdom, and the weariness, the jadedness, and the boredom of our contemporary culture testify to the futility and emptiness of worldly ways.

"Happy are the poor in spirit...

"Happy are those who mourn...

"Happy are the meek...

"Happy are those who hunger and thirst for righteousness...

"Happy are those who are persecuted..."

— Matthew 5:3-10

— 5 —

We take physical laws seriously: gravity, aerodynamics, etc.

We research them, conform to them, cooperate with them.

And in so doing we make fantastic technological progress: satellites in space, photographing the solar system, putting a man on the moon…

We provide artificial joints and organs for the human body, and even make test tube babies because we understand and obey physical laws.

Yet we function in *exactly the opposite way when it comes to spiritual and moral laws!* We ignore them, demean them, and disobey them.

Law-abiding when it comes to physical laws, we are lawless when it comes to the spiritual and moral order.

So we make incredible progress technologically… *and regress tragically in spiritual and moral matters*.

Result?

Children sexually active, exploited and destroyed… pregnancies are highest with children 9 to 15… abortions by the hundreds of thousands, adding infanticide to our depraved culture… sexual aberration is commonplace, accepted and promoted.

Alcoholism, drug abuse, and suicide are increasing epidemically.

And over everything, *technological progress threatens the survival of the human race.*

A highly scientific society and a morally degenerate culture. We are technological giants, spiritual and moral dwarfs…

"Because they exchanged the truth about God for a lie and worshipped and served the creature rather than the Creator, God gave them up to dishonorable passions. Their women exchanged natural relations for unnatural, and the men likewise gave up natural relations with women and were consumed with passion for one another, men committing shameless acts with men and receiving in their own persons the due penalty of their error."

— Romans 1:25-27

Conversion means change… *change of mind*:

About Myself: I'm tired of being the center of my existence; tired of being the reason for everything I think and say and do. Tired of being a neat little package all wrapped up in myself; tired of spinning like a top around my own ego — treating myself like my own little god, bowing down and worshipping me, myself and I.

I need a new center. Life has polarized around self long enough. I need to get off the hook of pride; to be loose for somebody else, free to live for something bigger than "number one."

About Sin: I'm fed up with my shallow excuses, making everybody else the scape-goat for my failure. Sick to the stomach with my deceitful rationalizing, my compulsive self justification… weary with the obsession to adjust to the sick society around me…

Nauseated with the pressure to conform; of being a moral chameleon; of blending into the limbo of contemporary culture… colorless, drab, meaningless.

My soul hungers for righteousness; for moral and spiritual health; for inward sanity, cleansing, wholeness, and vigor!

About Jesus Christ: He is what I need! His virtuous life with its balanced perfection, however you look at Him, by whatever criteria He is judged, is the object of my highest aspiration. He is my goal — my God!

He was filled with love and it kept spilling out all around Him. Let some of it spill on me, burn through me with holy fire, purge me — purify me.

He epitomized peace… how desperately my heart languishes for His peace. Not just peace of mind, the peace of the graveyard, or the peace of narcotics. Not the peace of compromise and slavery, co-existence with evil and filth, appeasement of the devil. *My soul demands the peace of Jesus Christ!*

Peace that enabled Him to sleep in a storm at sea when veteran mariners, hardened to the threat of wind and waves, quaked and quailed with fear. Peace that held in the midst of disappointment, fraud, hypocrisy, vicious hostility, tragedy. Peace that looked death in the eye and forced its retreat.

His violent death has meaning for me. He needn't have died, He could have escaped the cross — but He embraced it. He died for me.

About Life's Purpose: No longer will I live for self or money or fame. *I must live for the glory of God.* I give myself in unconditional surrender to Him to do His will. He is my Lord, I am His forever!

This is conversion! "Repent ye therefore and be converted."

— *Acts 3:19* ✠

If you're going to fight
Fight for the relationship — not against it!
Fight for reconciliation — not for alienation.
Fight to preserve the friendship — not to destroy it.
Fight to win your spouse — not to lose him/her.
Fight to save your marriage — not to cash it in.
Fight to solve the problem — not to Salve your ego.
If you're going to fight…
Fight to win — not to lose!
Lasting relationships are not negotiated — they are forged.
That means heat and pressure.

It is commitment to a relationship which sustains it — not pleasant feelings.

Treat a relationship as negotiable — it is easily lost.

Consider it non-negotiable — a way is found to make it work.

Authentic intimacy comes only through struggle.

"Love is patient and kind; love is not jealous or boastful; it is not arrogant or rude.

"Love does not insist on its own way; it is not irritable or resentful; it does not rejoice at wrong, but rejoices in the right.

"Love bears all things, believes all things hopes all things, endures all things.

"Love never ends."

— 1 Corinthians 13:4-8

8

Whence came I? Whither do I go? Why am I here?

Three basic questions that remain unanswered for so many.

A contemporary syndrome for both young and old.

An identity crisis.

How do you identify anything... a city for example?

By boundaries.

A football field? By boundaries. (It wouldn't be a game if it did not have to be played within boundaries.)

No boundaries, no identity... whether games or people.

"I do as I please" is the language of identity crisis...

As though limitations are evil.

That was the first temptation — the original one: God said, "Do not eat of that tree... if you do you will die." Satan contradicted, "You will not die."

Implicit in the contradiction was the lie — "God's limitations are evil. He is withholding something from you… don't allow God's restrictions to fool you and limit your freedom."

Our first parents believed the lie, ate the fruit… And lost their identity.

They passed the propensity to disbelieve God and to believe a lie down to their descendants in all future generations.

Hence our contemporary culture with its rejection of moral absolutes, its permissiveness, its unbelief, its "do your own thing" drifts in a milieu of meaninglessness, purposelessness and mindlessness…

Perishes in a spiritual vacuum.

"Let us hear the conclusion of the whole matter: Fear God, and keep his commandments, for this is the whole duty of man."

— *Ecclesiastes 12:13*

9

Quantity — or quality?

Two ways of thinking about life.

One person thinks in terms of quantity...

He judges everything by how big, how much, how high, how long.

He's generally happy when he has more of something than others.

His criteria for everything are materialistic.

He has little sense of the spiritual or the moral. He usually satiates his body and starves his soul.

Eternal values are unimportant — temporal values are everything!

The quality of what he produces is far less important than how much he makes in producing it.

He becomes increasingly more acquisitive and possessive, less and less loving, considerate, altruistic.

And with it all increasing insecurity, mistrust and fear attacks.

The wise view life qualitatively.

Priority is given to spiritual, moral, eternal values.

What he is is infinitely more important than what he has...

His relationships with his spouse, children, friends and peers take precedence over possessions.

He is concerned about what he produces — not just his profit.

He worships God.

"Indeed I count everything as loss because of the surpassing worth of knowing Christ Jesus my Lord."

— Philippians 3:8

High and dry."

Dry because high… That's the status of the proud one.

"High and dry."

High in ego — low in spirituality.

High in pride — low in moral courage and integrity.

High in self-righteousness — shriveled up in soul and spirit.

"Blessed are the poor in spirit, for theirs is the kingdom of heaven," said Jesus.

Symptom of lukewarmness in the Laodicean Church was precisely this. "Because Thou sayest, I am rich and increased with goods, and have need of nothing…"

— Revelation 3:17

"Need nothing?" *That's the abyss of faith.*

That is salt that has lost its savor.

As Jesus was unable to help the proud Pharisee impressed with his own piety, so Jesus can help no one who needs nothing.

In the most basic sense Christ came *for failures*.

There is no limit to what He can do for the one who humbles himself and asks for grace.

The mighty apostle Paul understood this: "My strength is made perfect in weakness… therefore I take pleasure in infirmities, because when I am weak then am I strong."

— 2 Corinthians 12:10

Begin low with Christ… *and the sky's the limit*.

"Whosoever shall exalt himself shall be abased; and he that humbleth himself shall be exalted."

— Matthew 23:12

"God resisteth the proud, and giveth grace to the humble."

— I Peter 5:5

— 11 —

We think we know where we are going.

In our technological, management-by-objective culture, we think we've got it all together.

We've got our goals — our objectives — our plans — our programs…

Our schedules.

And they've got us.

That's the dilemma — they've got us!

So we absolutize our Goals, sanctify our plans, idolize our programs, and bend to our schedules…

And forget God.

What's worse, our goals are not ends — they are all means.

All our ends are means.

We invest the best we have to offer of health and energy and time in that which is transitory.

We give our best to that which is temporal...

And ignore the eternal.

Abraham, the Father of the faith, "went out not knowing whither he went."

But "He looked for a city which hath foundations whose builder and maker is God."

— Hebrews 11:10

～ 12 ～

Putting no confidence in the flesh…"

The one who wrote those words also wrote, "If any other man thinks he has reason for confidence in the flesh, I have more…"

How is such a direct contradiction explained? How did the Apostle Paul justify it? By what process was this proud man humbled to a position so antithetical to one once held?

It began with a confrontation.

He was on his way to Damascus, chief persecutor of Christians, to imprison all he could.

In his religious zeal they represented a vicious heresy that demanded eradication and he was determined to do it.

He was proud of his religious achievements, *having exceeded all his peers by every standard raised* in his Judaistic faith.

"…as to righteousness under the law, blameless."

On his way to Damascus, this proud, self-righteous, morally superior man met Jesus Christ.

Jesus Christ, who had been crucified and buried long before, confronted this man in His resurrectionbody.

The belligerent enemy entered Damascus a *thoroughly devoted disciple* of the One whose followers he sought to exterminate.

He learned that it was his very religious pride and zeal that made him an enemy of the God he professed to worship… that true righteousness is a gift to be received, not a goal to be achieved… a truth preached by a prophet of Israel hundreds of years before: *"The just shall live by faith."*

So he testified how he found in Jesus Christ the authentic righteousness — and how his own energetic efforts to attain such righteousness had only resulted in making him an arrogant, self-righteous zealot.

"Indeed I count everything as loss because of the surpassing worth of knowing Christ Jesus my Lord. For His sake I have suffered the loss of all things, and count them as refuse, in order that I may gain Christ and be found in Him, not having a righteousness of my own, based on the law, but that which is through faith in Christ…"

— Philippians 3:8-9

13

C ynics do not create nations."

Nothing is less productive than cynicism.

Ultimately it hurts only the cynic — not the ones about whom he is cynical.

It is easy to justify cynicism — easy to find people in any category of human beings who are fakes, crooks, and liars.

You'll find them in all walks of life. All professions.

You find them among the clergy, even among journalists…

No group is without them.

There is so much greed and sin — in government, education, construction, medicine, business, industry, religion, labor, in the press.

It isn't difficult to find reason for cynicism.

Trouble is, the cynic is often blind to his own failure, as though he is separate or above the common crowd.

Or maybe he is cynical because of his own failure.

If he can't make it, why not tear down everybody who can?

Scapegoats are not hard to find!

Cynicism is utterly destructive.

Most of all, of the cynics!

"Judge not, that you be not judged. For with the judgment you pronounce you will be judged, and the measure you give will be the measure you get."

— *Matthew 7:1-2*

— 14 —

 reatness! God wants you to have it…

But not in the way of the world.

Constraint, modesty and submission are the ways of God to greatness…
ostentation, boasting and overbearance are the ways of the world.

Want to be great? Become the servant of all.

It is impossible to use humility to attain greatness in the worldly sense.

If you truly humble yourself, it will only lead to further humility.

When Jesus taught that the humble would be exalted, He was not disclosing
the secret to "one-up-manship."

This becomes clear when we understand the meaning of exaltation.

To be exalted means to be "lifted up."

Jesus used the same word in reference to His crucifixion:

"If I be lifted up (exalted), I will draw all men to myself."

Literally, Jesus is saying: "Whoever humbles himself will be exalted...
lifted up... crucified."

You can't avoid being exalted if you humble yourself.

But your elevation before man will be a kind of cross to bear...

It will be an exaltation of mortification.

"Humble yourself therefore under the mighty hand of God, that in due time
He may exalt you."

— I Peter 5:6

— 15 —

The most insidious temptation is not to evil…

It is the temptation to virtue!

This was, in fact, the original temptation.

Imagine the serpent saying to our first parents, "Don't believe what God says… listen to me, eat the fruit and go to hell."

Such an obvious suggestion would have no lure in it — the master deceiver is too shrewd for that!

First he questioned God's word: "Hath God said?" (The devil is relentless as the Bible's detractor.)

Next he contradicted God: "You will not die…"

Finally he turned the act of disbelieving and disobeying God into a desirable result: "Eat the fruit and you will be like God, knowing good from evil."

The temptation was to God likeness… and to this day man's greatest temptation is to be his own god — the ultimate expression of which is atheism.

"Man is god!"

This is the devil's masterpiece — leading people to believe that the way to be God-like is by human effort; that God-likeness is possible by human achievement.

In other words, heed the devil, believe and obey him... and be like God.

The supreme manifestation of this deception is humanism — man's belief in himself — man finding God unnecessary — man making it on his own. *This is the way of total destruction.*

Add technology to humanism and you've got the most deceptive form of human rebellion against God.

Humanism says, "We can do it." Technology says, "We'll give you the tools." This combination is the principal threat to human survival!

God says, "All have sinned and come short of the glory of God... God commendeth his love for us in that while we were yet sinners, Christ died for us... The blood of Jesus Christ, God's Son, cleanseth from all sin."

The ultimate choice: Believe what God says — or believe the devil.

A vindictive spirit is like a stone in the heart, blocking out the forgiveness of God.

The one who will not forgive cannot be forgiven.

Not that God will not forgive, but the unforgiving one is not receptive to His forgiveness.

When a person will not forgive another, he prevents himself from enjoying the forgiveness of God.

God's love and grace are available — but the unforgiving one, preoccupied with the offense to himself, is not receptive to God's mercy.

Unforgiveness is like a cancer that spreads among people.

Alienation between the offender and the offended does not stop with them — it infects the lives around them, enlarging and deepening the alienation.

In severe cases it forces people to take sides when they feel no enmity. Their friendship with one or the other coerces them into identifying with the aggrieved or the aggriever.

What begins as simple enmity between two grows and hardens.

Unforgiveness is like poison to one's soul!

The one who holds it suffers more than the one against whom revenge is nurtured.

Unforgiveness is antithetical to the spirit of Jesus Christ. Unforgiveness is antithetical to love. Unforgiveness is anti-social, anti-Christian, anti-human.

At the heart of unforgiveness is pride!

To forgive one must humble himself — which is difficult to do.

But it is the way of release — liberty — joy — love.

"If you forgive men their trespasses, your Father in Heaven will forgive you; but if you will not forgive men their trespasses, neither will your Father in Heaven forgive you."

— Matthew 6:14-15

Often, if not always, the reason people refuse to believe the truth about God is that they don't want to do it.

Evidence for faith is overwhelming — nevertheless they reject it.

Because *they will not obey.*

They rationalize their nonbelief, invent numerous intellectual reasons, resort to hypothetical questions, reduce arguments to an absurdity if necessary...

Anything to justify their rejection of truth.

But *the real reason is that they do not want to accept the implications and responsibility of belief.*

They will not obey God.

Some despise the moral restraints of God — others use their morality as a cover for not needing God.

Some create their own god — in their image — and find it easier to accept their homemade god as a substitute for Truth.

Some worship Nothing (with a capital "N").

They believe in No-God.

Human nature is very clever at avoiding God, rejecting God, rebelling against His will.

You see this manifested vividly in the New Testament record...

Everything about Jesus amazed the people. He spoke with authority, though He had no earthly credentials (He was just a carpenter). His learning was impressive, though He had not studied in their schools. His claims concerning Himself were startling, His works miraculous.

Even His enemies had to employ false witnesses in their attempt to discredit Him. And most rejected Him, finally crucifying Him.

"If any one will do God's will, he shall know the truth."

— *John 7:17*

ategories and caricatures…

The way of contemporary judgments…

False perceptions…

Everybody is stereotyped!

Put people in a category: teacher, clergy, doctor, lawyer, corporation executive, laborer, politician, policeman, salesman, etc.

Persons are no longer Perceived as they truly are — *distinct from all others*.

Lump everybody together in a category. Accept the cartoonist's caricature of the category.

And quit thinking.

Many years ago, a respected friend used to say,

"75% never think."

"15% think they think but they're only rearranging their prejudices."

"10% really think."

My impression is that the statistic is accurate. Non-thinking is endemic.

Even Jesus Christ is stereotyped.

"What think ye of Christ?"

— *Matthew 22:42*

"Come now and let us reason together, said the Lord."

— *Isaiah 1:18*

— 19 —

OALS!

Who dares challenge the concept?

It is virtually heresy to question the idea of goals. In the church as well as in business.

So?

Goals must be measurable — how else does one know how he is progressing toward his goal?

Which means results must be visible. . .

And quantifiable.

Which means *criteria must be materialistic*.

Size — numbers — dollars.

The "success" syndrome.

Spiritual values subject to materialistic judgments.

This is not to suggest that quantity is evil, or unnecessary...

But it is to argue that there is much in life that lies infinitely beyond any human measurement.

The highest values simply cannot be quantified!

"It is required in stewards that one be found faithful..."

Remember the words of the writer of Hebrews 11:13: "These all died in faith, not having received what was promised, but having seen it and greeted it from afar..."

"(Moses) endured as seeing Him who is invisible."

— Hebrews 11:27

~ 20 ~

Do you believe God... or just your beliefs about Him?

Here's the difference between what one has called "bumptious security" and authentic Christian assurance:

Nobody is surer than a fanatic!

He's absolutely, unshakably convinced in what he believes. In fact, that's precisely what makes him a fanatic. His views are final!

He's so convinced in his beliefs that he has stopped thinking.

At best, he just rearranges his prejudices.

The true Christian believes God...

Even though he is not sure of God's ways — because God "works in mysterious ways his wonders to perform" and God is therefore unpredictable.

Fanaticism is predictable, and because it is, the one who is so limited finds life to be increasing monotony and boredom.

Righteousness is unpredictable. This does not mean that it is erratic. Righteousness is absolutely consistent, trustworthy, logical... but by Divine, not human standards.

The true Christian is certain of God — though uncertain of what God will do next.

But absolutely certain that whatever God does is right, perfectly right.

For this reason, therefore, *the authentic Christian life is an adventure* filled with thrilling expectancy. Expectancy in God and His righteous overrule of life.

The Christian may not know the way, but he knows the One Who is ordering his steps.

He does not know what to expect, but he does know that whatever it is, it will "work out for good to those who love God, who are called according to His purpose."

He knows that life is a risk — but he has risked his life with God!

"If God be for us — who can be against us?"

— *Romans 8:31*

21

Tradition vs. truth! A relentless contest!

How easily human tradition replaces God's truth!

The Old Testament people of God did it... *and the New Testament People of God are no different.*

Both liberal and conservative in Jesus' day had traded the Word of God for their tradition.

The Sadducees had written off resurrection and eternal life.

The Pharisees had written off crucifixion... and reduced their religion to multitudes of rules — many of them trivial.

Their Messiah was to be a military hero and a political Savior.

Hence Peter's instant rejection of Jesus' comment about his suffering (Matt. 16:22) — despite his clear testimony to Jesus' Messiahship (Matt. 16:18).

Crucifixion did not conform to the traditional Messianic hope.

Which explains the sadness of the two men on the road to Emmaus.

"But we trusted..." they said. What sad words!

Which is why — after three intimate years with Jesus, and forty days with Him following His resurrection — their preoccupation was: "Lord, wilt thou at this time restore again the kingdom to Israel?"

— Acts 1:6

And what of we evangelicals today? Do we hold to the truth of God or is our preoccupation our tradition?

Are we expecting a political kingdom...

Or are we looking for Jesus' return?

"And Jesus said to them, 'Full well ye reject the commandment of God, that ye may keep your own tradition.'"

— Mark 7:9

22

Order is fundamental to human identity.

When order is transgressed humanness is violated.

The Ten Commandments are the basic order for authentic humanness.

They are not the arbitrary rules of a petty deity who wanted to "pull rank" or "throw his weight around" or show who's boss...

They are the fullest expression of humanness at its best — as it was intended by God in creation.

Long before they were engraved on tablets of stone by the "finger of God" and given to Moses — *they were written on the human heart.*

"When Gentiles who have not the law do by nature what the law requires... they show that what the law requires is written on their hearts."

— Romans 2:14-15

The Bible is not an archaic book of ancient myths and fables.

It is like an operator's manual that comes from the factory containing the manufacturer's directions on how to put the product together and make it work as intended.

Stop to think about it — the Ten Commandments are a perfect statement of human rights.

As they are broken human rights are violated.

The breakdown of our social order is no mystery — it is the direct result of a permissive culture in which morals are relative and ethics are situational.

Neither humans nor their institutions can withstand disregard for the moral absolutes of God.

Humanness is deformed and its institutions disintegrate when God's order is ignored and forsaken…

Which underlies the futility of legislation and education in their efforts to restore our society.

Humanism simply does not work — a fact to which history profoundly testifies.

"The times of ignorance God overlooked, but now He commands all men everywhere to repent, because he has fixed a day on which He will judge the world in righteousness."

— Acts 17:30

Be what you are!"

Simple…

But the fact is — many of us find it difficult to accept this as fundamental.

We keep trying to be what we are not — what we were never intended to be.

Life is a constant battle against built-in limitations.

Like trying to be a concert artist when one cannot sing.

Instead of accepting ourselves as we are.

As God made us to be…

We struggle to be like somebody else.

Somebody with different talents and gifts…

Somebody God intended to be unique.

Intimidated by the seeming superiority of another we ignore our uniqueness.

Meanwhile we sacrifice what we are.

One will never become what he can be...

Until he accepts what he is!

That's reality.

You are the only you God gave to our world... be yourself.

Don't deprive the world of you.

The apostle Paul knew the secret: "I am the least of the apostles, not fit to be called an apostle, because I persecuted the church. Nevertheless by the grace of God I am what I am."

— I Corinthians 15:10

I t doesn't take a big person to be used of God...

But it takes all there is of him!

You don't need a five-foot pipeline to irrigate a garden...

You can do it with a quarter-inch hose...

Assuming an adequate source — a connection between it and the hose — and an uncluttered channel.

The only ability God requires is availability.

Because the resources are His — and they are unlimited.

In His providence He pours those resources through human channels who are willing to be used.

Actually human ability can be a liability...

Because the able person trusts his own adequacy, his own resources, his own talent — and does not rely on God.

The power is God's...

The grace is God's...

The love is God's!

Inexhaustible power — grace and love ready to work through anyone who is available, who makes the connection of faith in Christ, who refuses to allow sin to clutter up his life.

That is the prospect for any person who desires it and yields to Christ, allowing the Holy Spirit of God to do the work of Christ through Him.

"Truly, truly, I say to you, he who believes in me will also do the works that I do; and greater works than these will he do...."

— *John 14:12*

"Now unto him *that* is able to do exceeding abundantly above all that we ask or think, according to the power that worketh in us."

— *Ephesians 3:20*

— 25 —

The hero does not set out to be one.

He is probably more surprised than others by such recognition.

He was there when the crisis occurred...

And he responded as he always had in any situation.

He was simply doing what had to be done!

Faithful where he was in his duty there...

He was ready when the crisis arose...

Being where he was supposed to be...

Doing what he was supposed to do...

Responding as was his custom...

To circumstances as they developed...

Devoted to duty — *he did the heroic.*

"Never allow the thought, 'I am of no use where I am,' you certainly are of no use where you are not."

— Oswald Chambers in *My Utmost for His Highest.*

"It is required in stewards that a man be found faithful."

— I Corinthians 4:2

ant to be a winner?

Compete against yourself… not somebody else.

Winning over another in golf doesn't mean you've shot your best game…

Winning a race against another doesn't mean you've run your best race.

You can beat another and still not fulfill your potential.

Which is as true in life as in sports.

To be your best you must compete with yourself.

The one who stops maturing spiritually because he thinks he knows more scripture than others or is doing better in other aspects, may be far from the most Christ has planned for him.

If you must compare yourself with another, compare yourself with Christ.

And let Him mold and fashion your life into the full potential...

The divine original He intends.

Become yourself, distinct from all others, as you allow Christ to control your life.

"Not as though I had already attained, either were already perfect; but I follow after, that I may apprehend that for which also I am apprehended of Christ Jesus... I press toward the mark for the prize of the high calling of God in Christ Jesus."

— *Philippians 3:12,14*

27

uccess in a venture does not necessarily constitute Divine favor... It may witness only to human ingenuity and efficiency. And it may result in human pride.

God often works through human failure.

Not that one seeks to fail...

But when sincere effort fails, *God may work in it to accomplish His purpose.*

And the glory will be God's!

Passion to succeed may interfere with the Spirit's direction...

Blind us to our need of God and dependence upon Him...

Drive us stubbornly in the way of carnality and disobedience.

When such passion is rewarded with success, it becomes easier to go on in the energy of the flesh. ("Nobody argues with success.")

Results, therefore, are not necessarily a valid criterion. They may be misleading... and dangerous.

To quote a familiar saying, *"God's work must be done God's Way to enjoy God's blessing."*

Jacob was remarkably capable and clever and shrewd.

His early life was an extraordinary record of achievement over father, brother, and father- in-law.

He won most of his battles, became very rich, and even won a wrestling match with God (Genesis 32: 25). But his real triumph came with a limp — and Jacob, nor his progeny, would ever forget that triumph.

Jacob's limp was a vivid reminder of his need of God. And his name was changed... he became Israel — "prince with God."

Do you have a limp?

"Not by might, nor by power, but by my Spirit, says the Lord."

— Zechariah 4:6

28

No one is so cocky as the one who doesn't know what he doesn't know.

One physicist, trying to explain the relationship between mass and space, said that if he could compress a person into solid mass he could put him into a thimble.

In fact, he said he could put the whole human race into the thimble that way.

In a single speck of dust there are more atoms than there are people in the world.

And the atom is divisible — a little universe — a "world of frantic, whirling movement... an association of electrons moving freely around a nucleus."

"The electron of an hydrogen atom rotates around its nucleus six thousand million million times in a single second."

Trying to comprehend a few simple facts about the atom reveals how impossible for our finite minds to understand the infinitesimal...

How much more impossible to comprehend infinity.

Which is why true intelligence and humility belong together.

The more one knows, the more he realizes he does not know. As knowledge increases, one's awareness of what lies beyond the known increases also.

The greater one's knowledge, the less he knows he knows compared to what remains unknown.

Said one great scientist, Sir Isaac Newton, late in life: "Here I stand on the edge of an ocean of truth. I have picked up a few grains of sand but the whole ocean lies beyond me unknown."

Faith and knowledge are not mutually exclusive. Faith begins with knowledge and goes beyond. *Life would be tragically limited if one could not live by faith.*

Reason is important — but it must keep its place.

The Bible is God's self-revelation… Jesus Christ is the Word of God made flesh. The wise one lives by faith in what the Bible says and what Jesus Christ has done.

"The just shall live by faith."

— Habakkuk 2:4

29

Jesus taught that "everyone who exalts himself will be humbled, and he who humbles himself will be exalted."

This is incontestably practical advice, even in a world where men manipulate people and things to obtain their own power and prestige, because there is always someone greater about to appear on the scene.

It may or may not be another person.

But it will always be Christ!

If we remember He is with us in every situation, we'll have little trouble making ourselves the least.

We can be satisfied to let God place us in circumstances with others who may be greater in position, gifts and talents because...

God will always arrange people in such a way as to give His Son the most prominence.

It works out this way because Christ has outdone us all in being the least.
"Do not put yourself forward in the King's presence
　　or stand in the place of the great;

　　　　for it is better to be told, 'Come up here,'

　　　　　　than to be put lower in the presence of the Prince."

— Proverbs 25:6,7

~~ 30 ~~

The man who knows where he is going is greatly admired in our culture. He is to be emulated.

The one who is sure of himself — who has "all his ducks in a row" — is considered an exemplary model in twentieth century America.

The one who has defined his goals, planned the strategy by which to achieve them, whose P.E.R.T. chart conforms to the plan… he is honored.

In our evangelical subculture, this is the way we tend to think. This is the kind of person we want most to be like.

Is it conceivable that this is worldliness, secularism, materialism in the most subtle and seductive sense?

Consider Abraham — giant of faith, father of the faithful — whose "seed" was to bless "…all the families of the earth."

"…he went out, not knowing where he was to go."

— Hebrews 11:8

"...he sojourned in the land of promise, as in a foreign land, living in tents."

— Hebrews 11:9

He was a nomad, a desert wanderer, as were "...Isaac and Jacob, heirs with him of the same promise."

— Hebrews 11:9

Abraham "...looked forward to a city which hath foundations, whose builder and maker is God."

— Hebrews 11:10

His hope lay beyond history.

He was the father of our faith — no better model as we look toward the new century.

"For my thoughts are not your thoughts, neither are your ways my ways, saith the Lord. For as the heavens are higher than the earth, so are my ways higher than your ways, and my thoughts than your thoughts."

— Isaiah 55:8,9

31

Independence is a wonderful word…

And the status God intended for man.

But that status maintains only as man lives *in dependence upon God*.

To be independent of God is to be finally dependent upon circumstances — and to be their victim.

To be authentically independent one must live in dependence upon God.

In his perfection as created by God, man was free — free even to disbelieve God and to reject His love and will.

In rejecting God's Word and will, man began to be bound.

Generation by generation throughout human history this bondage has deepened and hardened…

Except as God has visited man with spiritual awakening…

And man has renewed his submission to God — his dependence upon God.

Here is the paradox: in the freedom given by God, man is perfectly free... free even to rebel against God.

But in rebellion in the name of freedom, man imperils his liberty.

Bound to God man is perfectly free.

Independent of God man capitulates to bondage.

Bad habits illustrate the principle: One begins by doing as he pleases — against God's moral law — and soon is bound by the habit.

In the beginning one is free to do or not to do. But as he persists, the habit enslaves and *he is no longer free not to do.*

"Stand fast therefore in the liberty wherewith Christ has made us free."

— *Galatians 5:1*

32

If God gave you three wishes…

Just three…

What would they be?

If God should say to you, "I will give you anything you want in three wishes."

What would you want?

If you knew you had exhausted all possibilities in three wishes…

What would you request?

To put it another way — What do you really want in life?

What are your deepest aspirations — longings —desires?

The fact is, God looks at our desires more than our decisions…

Because desire is deeper than decision.

If God gave you three wishes…

Only three and no more…

What would they be?

"Take delight in the Lord, and He will give you the desires of your heart."

— *Psalm 37:4*

33

I t's safe to let Jesus Christ have the last word.

We get under pressure, begin to feel we have failed if we can't wrap up a discussion in a neat little package and tie the knot.

As though loose ends after a discussion are bad.

Like a high pressure auto salesman — we feel we have to "close" right now...

And we move the prospect forcefully into the "closing room."

Forcing a decision for Christ prematurely may abort...

The prospect may capitulate just to get you off his back.

You can leave a man safely in the hands of Christ after you have done your best with him.

You don't have to give him all the answers.

Give him air, let him think, allow the Holy Spirit to water the seed you've sown in his heart.

The Word of God is good seed — it has life in it.

Matter of fact, the finest strategy with a person may be to let him go without any attempt to finalize...

Let him go knowing he has been confronted by Christ and must answer to Him inevitably.

Let Christ have the last word.

"(My Word) shall not return unto me void..."

— Isaiah 55:11

34

Gratitude…

A shortened form for grateful attitude.

Which should characterize the disciple of Christ.

Why is it that we tend not to appreciate a blessing until we lose it?

I really didn't appreciate the blessing of walking until an arthritic hip made it almost impossible to walk and surgery was necessary.

Never had I appreciated the blessing of walking so much as when I was able to walk again without pain.

Nor did I appreciate sight until surgery was necessary for cataract removal and a detached retina.

Now every day I thank God for the freedom…
To walk…
And to see.
God help us so we don't have to lose blessings before we appreciate them.
"Be joyful always,
Pray continually,
Give thanks in all circumstances,
For this is God's will for you in Christ Jesus."

— *1 Thessalonians 5:16-17*

35

Prayer is not so much getting things from God…
As it is getting God's viewpoint about things.
It is seeking God's will rather than demanding my way.
It is submitting to God — not using God.

Prayer is as much listening to God as it is talking to God.

It is dialogue… not monologue!

It is waiting on God… not being in a hurry for God to do something.

Prayer is spending time with God for its own sake…

Not just asking and running.

Prayer is not "Gimmie — Gimmie — Gimmie."

It is "Lord, what wilt Thou have me to do?"

To say "Now!" to God is as presumptuous as to say "No!" to God.

It is of the mercy of God that He makes us wait... *or that He does not always give us what we ask for.*

Often we are like little children asking for machine guns or time bombs or high-powered rifles.

We're not equipped to use what we request.

Prayer's preoccupation is the glory of God's name... the doing of God's will on earth as in heaven... the coming of God's kingdom.

True prayer is simply to know God!

Jesus said, "When you pray say, 'Our Father, who art in heaven, hallowed be Thy name; Thy kingdom come, Thy will be done on earth as it is in heaven.' "

— Matthew 6:9,10

36

 sentence from a pastor's prayer recently suggests a fitting epitaph on the tombstone of our contemporary culture…

He prayed, "Forgive us, Lord…

"We seek to go faster and faster and faster… we accumulate more and more and more…

"But we find no meaning or satisfaction in speed or acquisition."

I thought…

We go faster and faster and faster…but we never seem to have enough time…and we never seem to get anywhere!

We acquire more and more and more… but we never seem to have enough… we never seem to be satisfied.

And we're rarely, if ever, thankful…

For time or possessions.

More never seems to be enough.

More! The obsession of a materialistic culture...

And its ultimate destruction.

Forgive us, Lord... we who always have more than enough of everything...

For our ingratitude — and our indifference to those who never have enough of anything;

And make us thankful.

"... for although they knew God, they did not honor Him as God, or give thanks to Him, but they became futile in their thinking and their senseless minds were darkened."

— Romans 1:21-22

Love is never wasted.

It may not get the results or the reaction that is expected…

But it is never wasted.

In fact, love that expects positive reaction or results is something less than love.

Love never makes any demands…

Love only gives…

And it does not cease when there is no reciprocity.

The true lover does not require the beloved to meet any conditions.

True love is unconditional.

The perfect lover devoted Himself to others…

And they crucified Him.

"This love of which I speak is slow to lose patience — it looks for a way to be constructive.

"It is not possessive: it is neither anxious to impress nor does it cherish inflated ideas of its own importance.

"Love has good manners and does not pursue selfish advantage.

"It is not touchy. It does not keep account of evil or gloat over the wickedness of other people. On the contrary, it is glad with all good men when truth prevails.

"Love knows no limit to its endurance, no end to its trust, no fading of its hope; it can outlast anything. It is in fact, the one thing that still stands when all else has fallen."

— 1 Corinthians 13: 4-8 J.B. Phillips Translation

"God commendeth his love toward us in that while we were yet sinners Christ died for us."

— Romans 5:8

"… if God so loved us, we ought to love one another."

— I John 4:11

— 38 —

Friendship!

What a beautiful, uncommon word!

Uncommon, not because it is rarely used…

Uncommon because it is rarely spoken in its profound sense.

And especially rare in the context of personal evangelism.

Most personal evangelism, as I have observed it for fifty years, is something you do to someone you don't know somewhere else than where you are.

Or something done to ("done to" used advisedly) someone with whom the personal evangelist has little relationship…

Certainly not friendship!

Tragically, not uncommonly the zealous personal evangelist ignores meaningful relationship with one who has refused to respond favorably to his evangelistic advances.

In fact, often the evangelistic approach alienates the "target."

Jesus was a "Friend of sinners."

Friend to the friendless… friend, even to His enemies!

What a difference when evangelism issues out of friendship and love.

How beautiful when one is loved to Christ… rather than being an object sought after as a means to achieve some evangelistic goal or record.

"He who loves is born of God and knows God. He who does not love does not know God."

— *1 John 4:7-8*

39

Relationships are not nurtured through negotiation… if anything they are strained!

In negotiation each side gives as little as necessary… gets as much as possible…

Then waits for the next round in hope of getting more…and giving less than the time before.

Recovering what was traded earlier is the strategy.

Negotiation generates competition, never cooperation… perpetuates adversaries, never produces a team.

In negotiation to lead from strength is fundamental.

Vulnerability is to be avoided at all cost… to be vulnerable is bad business in our culture.

Good relationships come through love and forgiveness… somebody has to be vulnerable, to lead from weakness, to give in, to lose.

That is repulsive to human ego and human pride.

Good relationships are not based on the 50/50 principle...

Someone has to be willing to go all the way... all the time.

What is of greater value than secure relationships? How often do we trade in a good relationship for trivia?

Love and forgiveness are costly... but they are the price of good relationships between husbands and wives, parents and children, blacks and whites, neighbors and friends.

Which is why it is so easy to talk peace... and so costly to have it.

Peace talkers are a dime a dozen... peace makers are rare and priceless.

Jesus Christ is the perfect model. *He never negotiated.* He loved. He gave and gave and gave... all the way to the cross.

Relationship begins when somebody leads from weakness!

"If God so loved us, we ought to love one another."

— I John 4:11

40

Lost!"

A strong biblical word that has little if any meaning for many these days. It has to do with humanness. It involves human orientation.

Man was made for fellowship with God — sin in its root sense is a broken relationship with God.

Humanness is realized only in a right relationship with God.

Out of fellowship with God, man is disoriented...

That is, he is lost!

Reality — sanity — meaning — purpose — identity — fulfillment — are all involved in human lostness.

Out of fellowship with God, life is unreal...

Meaningless...

Purposeless...

Empty...

Non-fulfilling.

It is to be satiated yet unsatisfied.

It is to suffer a profound hunger — thirst — longing — loneliness — alienation — which only God can satisfy.

Sin is man's self-alienation from God; human rejection of God's love and grace; the voluntary disconnection from ultimate reality.

To be lost is to be sub-human — less than intended — out of touch — in limbo.

To remedy this situation Jesus Christ entered history…

And that's what Christianity is all about. *You can have a relationship with God!*

"I tell you the truth, whoever hears my word and believes Him who sent me has eternal life and will not be condemned; he has crossed over from death to life."

— John 3:16

41

Think of the tremendous relief that comes with the word of a trustworthy friend...

The child who is fearful in the dark until it hears the familiar voice of a parent saying, "Don't be afraid, I'm here."

The loneliness that is dispelled when a voice over the phone speaks reassurance.

The incredible relief when there's been an accident and the phone rings and the voice says, "I'm okay."

The extraordinary power of words to restore confidence.

A big bill is due in a week and there's no money to pay...

The need is shared with a friend who says, "Don't give it another thought, I'll see that you have the money on time."

Anxiety vanishes — the matter is taken care of — with profound relief gratitude is expressed as the burden is lifted…

Not because the money has been given, but because it has been promised.

The word of a trusted friend now removes the worry of a future problem.

So God's word relieves…

When it is taken seriously!

The trouble is, we are unfamiliar with His word — or if we know it we don't believe it or accept it.

Growing spiritually is learning to know — and trust — God's word.

"Faith comes by hearing and hearing by the word of God."

— Romans 10:17

our solid facts upon which to build your life:

God knows you!

From Him you have no secrets. He knows all about you — your weakness and inadequacy, your sin, your failure.

"0 Lord, thou hast searched me and known me. Thou knowest when I sit down and when I rise up; thou discernest my thoughts from afar and art acquainted with all my ways."

— Psalm 139:1-3

God loves you!

He loves you unconditionally — unwaveringly — everlastingly — relentlessly.

God is love. "Nothing can separate us from the love of God which is in Jesus Christ our Lord."

— Romans 8:39

God cares for you!

"Do not be anxious about your life, what you shall eat or what you shall drink, nor about your body, what you shall put on. Look at the birds of the air: they neither sow nor reap nor gather into barns, and yet your heavenly Father feeds them. Are you not of more value than they?"

— Matthew 6:25-26

God has a plan for your life!

"You saw me before I was born and scheduled each day of my life before I began to breathe."

— Psalm 139:16, Living Bible

But God will not impose His will upon you. He will not coerce. It is up to you to accept or reject... His knowledge of you — His love — His care — His plan.

"God so loved the world that He gave His only begotten Son that whoever believes in Him shall not perish but have everlasting life."

— John 3:16

43

He is a much respected Bible teacher and shall remain unnamed. For years he has had my admiration, respect and affection. It was, therefore, difficult to accept a recent lesson on prayer.

"We pray for daily provision," he said, speaking about the simple petition in the Lord's prayer, "give us this day our daily bread."

But he went on to insist that "God did not want us to be dressed poorly, or to be driving around in a run-down automobile" — and the litany continued, corresponding to our present-day culture.

My mind went immediately to Ethiopia and Somalia, where some of God's children subsist on roots and leaves.

Bangladesh — Haiti — Calcutta flashed into my mind with vivid memories of indescribable poverty and tragedy.

And to precious sisters and brothers in Christ who live in Washington's inner city.

I remembered a guest we had in our home during a Christmas holiday. He was a student from Burma, a Presbyterian pastor whose monthly income was about $100.

He owns no automobile, must walk wherever he goes in his pastoral duties. He has few books or other possessions... but he is a radiant follower of Christ.

How easily we equate our lifestyle in this upper middle class culture with Biblical truth... yet what disparity between such thinking and Biblical teaching.

We are 6% of the world's peoples and we consume nearly 50% of the world's goods.

Which ought to concern us deeply...

But what is worse: we assume that our incredible abundance is normal for all human beings, *and even sanctify such an assumption with the Bible.*

"Lay not up for yourselves treasures upon earth, where moth and rust doth corrupt, and where thieves break through and steal; but lay up for yourselves treasures in Heaven, where neither moth nor rust doth corrupt, and where thieves do not break through nor steal."

— Matthew 6:19-20

~ 44 ~

U pon observing a blade of grass breaking through a slab of concrete, it is said that Albert Einstein was inspired with the following advice to an anxious colleague…

"Bloom where you are planted!"

Whether or not Einstein coined this saying, it is a profound statement of faith. *God intends that we blossom where planted.*

Jesus teaches that, "…Unless a grain of wheat falls into the earth and dies, it remains alone…but if it dies, it bears fruit."

— John 12:24

If we are to be fruitful, we must die to ourselves, part of which means to be accepting of, rather than objecting to, the God-given people and circumstances into which we are thrown each moment.

To walk by faith is to believe that our daily routine is a "furrow" to be sown into, rather than a "rut" to get out of.

As we allow ourselves to be buried in the soil of each worldly predicament, we inevitably break through and reap a harvest.

Here and now, we may as well trust that we are of the most use where we are. To quote another: "We are certainly of no use where we are not!"

As you walk into your next situation — no matter how overwhelming — remember:

You go nowhere by mistake — The Lord leads you.

You go nowhere alone — He is with you.

You go nowhere unprepared — He is in you.

"The one who sowed the good seed is the Son of Man. The field is the world, and the good seed stands for the sons of the kingdom."

— *Matthew 13:37*

⟿ 45 ⟾

The tragedy is not that a man suffers…

But that he suffers for nothing — or for an unworthy cause.

Suffering is inescapable — an ingredient of life — a stubborn fact.

Suffering cannot be avoided by pretending it does not exist.

Evasion is weakness — not wisdom. Ignoring the reality does not eliminate the problem.

The choice is not whether a man will suffer… *but what he suffers for.*

Some men suffer to make a success in business or a career.

Some suffer to make a million dollars.

Others suffer to become famous, or popular, or powerful… to gain position or influence or prestige.

Suffering is the stuff of human greatness, the raw material of character when taken rightly…

It gives dimension to life: depth, understanding, strength, soundness.

It sweeps the shallowness out of life.

Of course a man may grow bitter through suffering... but this only compounds the tragedy; makes suffering doubly disastrous, and causes it to hurt twice.

Embittered by suffering, a man turns hard and brittle...

And usually the man embittered by suffering is the one who suffers for a worthless cause... or no cause at all.

Suffering is meaningless, purposeless, because he has no standards, no principles, no worthy goals... nothing to die for... or live for!

The man who lives for a cause worthy enough to die for makes suffering serve him — serve his high purpose. And suffering becomes a bona fide asset.

Peter Marshall said, "It is better to fail in a cause that will ultimately succeed, than to succeed in a cause that will ultimately fail."

"Endure suffering as a good soldier of Jesus Christ."

— 2 Timothy 2:3

46

The world and all that is in the world" constitutes a very strong, almost irresistible gravity pull on the people of God.

Tension between *what is* and *what is to be* is at times almost unendurable.

It's tempting to trade future hope for present satisfaction...

It's so easy to settle for half best now rather than best later.

The absolute is so easily turned in for the relative... the eternal for the temporal.

Egypt, despite its slavery, pulled so relentlessly on the children of Israel that they complained constantly to Moses... and were tempted often to forsake the land of milk and honey.

How compelling the present — the earthly — the best possible here and now rather than the perfect city of God.

Some years ago, Malcolm Muggeridge was a guest at a breakfast in Washington at which he gave the story of his "rediscovery of Jesus."

He spoke about world conditions, and he sounded very pessimistic.

A brother questioned him, "Dr. Muggeridge, you have been so pessimistic, are you not optimistic about anything?"

"My friend," replied Muggeridge, "I could not be more optimistic than I am, for my hope is in Jesus Christ and Him alone!"

There was heavy silence for some seconds. Then Muggeridge continued, "Just suppose that the apostolic church had put its hope in the Roman Empire?"

Think!

In whom do we trust?

"Jesus answered, 'My kingdom is not of this world; if my kingdom were of this world, then would my servants fight, but now is my kingdom not from hence.'"

— John 18:36

47

Homesickness...

A common malady that every one of us has felt at one time or another.

It can be very painful.

In the deepest sense it is the most fundamental need humans experience.

We are homesick for God!

We were created for fellowship with God... made for a right relationship with Him.

Humanness suffers radically when this relationship is broken.

Alienation from God is destructive of human nature — its inevitable by-product is inhumanity.

Self-alienation from God is sin in the profoundest sense.

All sins, all human disorders, all human caricatures, all sickness, all other alienations derive from it as fruit from seed.

Jesus Christ entered history to reconcile man to God.

His life, His words, His work were for this single purpose.

His supreme work was His death on the cross as the sacrifice for sin.

His resurrection was the Father's total satisfaction of that work.

Rejection of Christ is the most common symptom of man's self-alienation from God.

Acceptance of Christ's work and obedience to Christ's word are the way to reconciliation and authentic humanness.

"My people have committed two evils," says the Lord. "They have forsaken me, the fountain of living waters, and hewed out cisterns for themselves, broken cisterns, that can hold no water."

"If any one thirst, let him come to me and drink. He who believes in me, as the scripture has said, 'Out of his heart shall flow rivers of living water.' "

— *John 7:37,38*

48

I t is wrong to ignore and neglect the hunger, nakedness and oppression of people in zeal to save them from hell.

But it is infinitely worse to satisfy their hunger and nakedness and let them go to hell!

It is unlike Christ not to care for the poor, the persecuted, the oppressed.

But it is a denial of Christ to care only for their physical need and ignore their eternal welfare.

He cared for the poor and oppressed…

But He came "to seek and save those who were lost."

In His life He ministered to the blind, the crippled, the sick, and the needy…

But in His death He purchased their eternal salvation.

He was a Servant — a teacher — a Prophet...

But He was also "the Lamb of God that taketh away the sin of the world."

Followers of Christ ought to be like their Lord in compassionate response to human need...

But they repudiate their Lord if they do not give priority to their eternal salvation.

Jesus said, "...do not fear those who kill the body, and after that have no more that they can do. Fear him who, after he has killed, has power to cast into hell."

— Luke 12:5

49

There's something worse than contempt for property...

Contempt for persons.

So far as Jesus Christ is concerned, you cannot pile enough property together to equal the value of one person...

Any person!

Jesus didn't love property...

He loved people... and used property.

We tend to use people... and love property.

Jesus did not die for property. *He died for people!*

Property has its place in the Christian view of life.

It is to be treated as a trust from God.

It requires careful stewardship.

It is to be used to the glory of God… and the benefit of persons!

Handled any other way it becomes a curse.

The value of one person… any person…

Is incalculable.

All the wealth of the world does not add up to the worth of one person!

"What shall it profit a man if he gain the whole world and lose his own soul? What shall a man give in exchange for his soul?"

— *Mark 8:36,37*

50

A friend writes, "I guess I have a typical case of 'I believe — but I doubt.' I doubt that God is guiding me regarding my future.

"For the past five years my job history has been quite poor — not by my choice, but by circumstances I had little to do with. No doubt my faith has grown with these experiences, but when does it stop?

"Naturally I want some security with a happy job but when does this, if ever, come about? I'm grateful for health, family, and everything, but boy, does it get frustrating regarding this employment thing."

What does one do in such a situation?

He begins by accepting the fact of his circumstances as they are.

One of the hardest things we have to do is accept things as they are... but that is the only solid foundation for growth and progress.

We keep trying to build on things as we wish they were...

That's like starting to build from the top down.

The dreams keep collapsing.

You cannot begin where you are not!

Wherever you are, however difficult it is, however adverse the circumstances — that's where you must begin.

That's where God will begin with you!

The Apostle Paul knew the secret...

He wrote, "I have learned in whatsoever state I am, therein to be content..." He also said, "... by the grace of God I am what I am."

He didn't resign himself to the status quo, nor did he resent reversals. He rejoiced in whatever his circumstances were in the conviction that God was leading.

Favorable circumstances do not necessarily indicate Divine favor... *nor do unfavorable circumstances indicate Divine displeasure.*

God's promise to lead — despite the circumstances — is all we need. That's the way of faith!

educe life to simplest terms and it is a matter of relationship.

God created man for fellowship with Himself.

God "saw that it was not good for man to be alone so He created woman" to complement or complete man.

The relationship between the man and his wife was designed by God to be the perfect human analogy of God's relationship with man (Read Ephesians 5:21-33).

Life is right when relationships are right — life suffers when relationships are broken.

Sin destroys relationships.

In disobeying God man ruptured fellowship with God and all human relationships have suffered since.

All alienation — whether between nations or races or sexes or ages — *all alienation* between persons has its source in man's rejection of God's will.

Jesus Christ entered history as the great Reconciler…

His life, death and resurrection were for the purpose of reconciling man to God and man to man.

Not only did Jesus demonstrate God's love for man ("God commendeth his love to us in that while we were yet sinners Christ died for us."), His act of love on the cross provided the means whereby fellowship between man and God, and man and man, could be restored.

Man's rejection of God's love in Christ is confirmation of the depravity in man resulting from the disobedience of the first man.

Man says he wants peace but he chooses alienation by refusing the One Who brings reconciliation...

Man says he wants peace but he rejects the Prince of peace...

Which proves that there is something in man that prefers war to peace!

That is one explanation for the man who espouses peace and does violence in the process.

"God was in Christ reconciling the world unto Himself... therefore be reconciled to God."

— 2 Corinthians 5:19-21

52

Humanity is incurably religious…

We must believe in God or find a substitute.

Even if that substitute is a No god.

It takes great faith to believe in a No god!

If we will not worship the true God, we will find a replacement… or invent our own god.

But each of us needs some kind of a god.

And we become like the god we worship.

We grow inevitably into the image of the god we follow.

Worship wealth — become materialistic, greedy and hard.

Worship fame — become arrogant, proud and boastful.

Worship power — become thoughtless, selfish and manipulative.

Worship pleasure — become shallow, transparent and empty.

The prophet Jeremiah described it precisely...

"What wrong did your fathers find in me that they went far from me, and went after worthlessness and became worthless?"

— Jeremiah 2:5

Another translation: "Following after hollow gods, they became hollow souls."

"...My people have committed two evils: they have forsaken me, the fountain of living waters, and hewed out cisterns for themselves, broken cisterns that can hold no water."

— Jeremiah 2:13

53

Order is freedom. Disorder is bondage!

Moral permissiveness in the name of personal freedom is delusion of the greatest magnitude.

To live on the basis of "I do as I please" is to court disaster.

Imagine a football game without any rules...

It wouldn't last ten minutes! (If anyone would even bother to get involved.)

Imagine a busy intersection downtown without traffic lights...

It would take hours to untangle the tie up.

And the longer it took the worse it would get as tempers were inflamed, people were trying to take matters into their own hands.

You see, *rules make the game.* Thousands enjoy playing the game, and multiplied thousands are thrilled as they watch it.

Rules are as basic to life as they are to games.

American life is governed by a moral order, instituted by God and agreed upon among men.

Man violates that order at his own peril.

Morality is not arbitrary… it is part of the natural law of the universe and as basic to life as gravity.

"For the wages of sin is death, but the gift of God is eternal life through Jesus Christ our Lord."

— *Romans 6:23*

54

There's a difference between church work and the work of the church.

Church work is being done when the church establishment is running its business.

When church work is being done, the church is fathered and visible...

When the work of the church is being done, the church is scattered and invisible.

When the church is gathered, it is being prepared for its work in the world...

Worship, preaching, music, teaching, pastoral ministry are all church work.

Church work involves its programs, organizations, and corporate plan...

The work of the church involves what the members of the church are doing between Sundays — business, industry, the professions, education, labor, agriculture, sales, consulting.

Like salt, the church is doing its work when scattered — when penetrating the food and becoming invisible.

Salt, when visible and confined in the salt shaker, is useless...

Like seed — useless when gathered in the granary — does its work when it is scattered, penetrating the soil, invisible.

"He that soweth the good seed is the son of man; the field is the world; the good seed are the children of the kingdom... the harvest is the end of the age; and the reapers are the angels."

— *Matthew 13:37-39*

55

What is man?

Naturalism says he is a product of a long evolutionary process.

Marxism says he has value only as he produces.

Secularism says he is important only as he achieves — and his importance is measured by his achievement.

Materialism says he is worth what he possesses.

In any case man has no value in and of himself — life has no meaning apart from usefulness; there is no such thing as human destiny.

According to the Bible man is of intrinsic worth. He was created by God in His image, to be loved by God, to be a friend of God, and to enjoy Him forever.

Man therefore is of infinite value!

Such value that the Son of God left heaven and came to earth to die on a cross so that man could live forever in his heavenly Father's presence and blessing.

The measure of the value of one person — any person — is the measure of Christ's sacrifice!

In the economy of God there is no such thing as an unimportant person! Each individual is precious — eternally precious to God!

"You created every part of me; you put me together in my mother's womb. I praise you because you are to be feared; all you do is strange and wonderful. I know it with all my heart.

"When my bones were being formed, carefully put together in my mother's womb, when I was growing there in secret, you knew that I was there — you saw me before I was born. The days allotted to me had all been recorded in your book, before any of them ever began."

— Psalm 139:13-16, Good News Bible

56

There's a world of difference between knowing about and knowing.
To know about is knowledge…
To know is experience.
To know about is cerebral…
To know is visceral — empirical — practical.
One may know about a person and not know him at all.
You may know a person — and know little about him.
Many of us know a great deal about Abraham Lincoln…
But we don't know him.

We may know much more about him than his most intimate friends knew...

But they knew him... we do not.

One may know a great deal about theology...

And not know God.

One may have much knowledge about the Bible without having had any personal experience with Jesus Christ.

Jesus was quite clear on this...

"And this is eternal life, that they know thee the only true God, and Jesus Christ whom thou hast sent."

— John 17:3

I watched the space shuttle make a perfect landing in the desert... concluding a successful mission.

Tens of thousands of man-hours — the finest in space science and the most sophisticated technology were involved...

As well as an investment of billions of dollars.

But it would have been impossible if there were not an orderly universe.

The best in space science, the most sophisticated technology would have been helpless...

If physical order could not have been counted on.

In fact, much of the genius of the plan, preparation and procedure involved the most precise knowledge of and conformity to the order.

Violation would have meant disaster!

Without order there would be no science!

God has ordained order in the moral and spiritual realms as well.

Conformity guarantees fulfillment...

Disobedience spells destruction.

The "law of sin and death" is as inviolate as the law of gravity.

"For the wages of sin is death, but the free gift of God is eternal life in Christ Jesus our Lord."

— Romans 6:23

J ustice in the biblical meaning is more than a legal term.

It's not just a matter of courts and judges, lawyers and litigation.

It has to do with righteousness… rightness between man and God, between man and man.

Justice has to do with distribution…

It is unjust for some always to have more than enough of everything while many never have enough of anything.

Justice means equitable distribution.

But justice also has to do with production.

To produce less than one is capable of is unjust.

To refuse to live up to one's full potential is a problem as much as it involves failure to distribute.

The fact is, God's initial mandate to humanity is precisely this...

"Be fruitful and multiply, and fill the earth and subdue it; and have dominion over... every living thing."

— Genesis 1:28

59

ho hasn't failed?

The apostle Paul failed... Peter failed... every one of twelve apostles failed.

David, Israel's greatest king, a man after God's own heart, failed.

Moses, giant among the Israelites, giver of the law, deliverer of is people... failed.

Jacob, father of Israel, failed. Isaac, son of the promise, failed. Abraham, progenitor of Israel, father of the faithful, prototype of those who are righteous through faith, failed.

Even our first parents, in their human perfection, failed.

Who hasn't failed?

It isn't failing that is the problem... *it's what one does after he has failed.*

To take failure as final is to be a failure... to see in failure the school of the Spirit is to let failure contribute to one's growth in Christ.

"To what do you attribute your success?" asked the young executive of the bank president he was to succeed.

"Two words," responded the president, "Good decisions."

"But how did you learn to make good decisions?" the young executive continued.

"One word," replied the president, "Experience."

"But how did you get the experience?" asked the young man.

"Two words," the president answered, "Bad decisions."

Who hasn't failed? Only one — Jesus Christ. And in His perfection He laid down His life to cover the failure of all.

"God works in everything for good to those who love Him, who are called according to His purpose."

— Romans 8:28

—ᴧᴧ 60 ᴧᴧ—

Justice has to do with ownership!

Who owns what you possess?

Your home, for example — does a Savings and Loan Company hold title?

Banks probably own some of your appliances, your car, perhaps part of your business.

In contemporary American culture, ownership can be very deceptive.

The land you say you own? It was there long before you were born.

It will be there long after you are gone.

Which illustrates ownership in the biblical-justice sense. God commanded Israel that all land was to be returned to its original boundaries in the Year of Jubilee — "The land shall not be sold in perpetuity, for the land is mine."

— Leviticus 25:23

"The earth is the Lord's, and the fullness thereof, the world and they that dwell therein."

— Psalm 24:10

"The silver is mine and the gold is mine, says the Lord of hosts."

— Haggai 2:8

"For every beast of the forest is mine, the cattle on a thousand hills."

— Psalm 40:10

Whatever we possess is a trust from God and we are accountable to Him as to its use.

This profound reality was one of the results of Pentecost, as well...

"Now the company of those who believe were of one heart and soul, and no one said that any of the things which he possessed was his own."

— Acts 4:32